AF480094

Ella and Daddy:

Can We Play Monster Now?

Written by: Brian Strickland | Illustrated by: Okko W

Daddy, can we play monster now?
Not now, I am working

I am
working

Daddy, can we play monster now?
Not now, I am cooking

I am
cooking

Not now,
I am cleaning
Daddy, can we play
monster now?

I am
cleaning

Daddy, can we play monster now?
Not now, I am relaxing

I am
Relaxing

Daddy, can we play monster now?
Not now, it is time for bed

Daddy, I am in bed

RRRRRROOOOOOAAARRR!!!!

I will
find you

Good night,
my little monster

The End

www.ingramcontent.com/pod-product-compliance
Lightning Source LLC
Chambersburg PA
CBHW042136110726
48006CB00003B/904